~WHEN~ DINOSAURS RULED ~THE~ EARTH

Rod Theodorou

Thomson Learning
New York

THE REMARKABLE WORLD

Dangerous Waters

MONSTERS OF THE DEEP
PIRATES AND TREASURE
VOYAGES OF EXPLORATION
THE WHALERS

Fearsome Creatures

BIRDS OF PREY
LAND PREDATORS
NIGHT CREATURES
WHEN DINOSAURS RULED THE EARTH

First published in the United States in 1996 by
Thomson Learning
New York, NY

Published simultaneously in Great Britain by Wayland
(Publishers) Ltd.

U.S. copyright © 1996 Thomson Learning

U.K. copyright © 1995 Wayland (Publishers) Ltd.

Library of Congress Cataloging-in-Publication Data
Theodorou, Rod.
When dinosaurs ruled the earth / Rod Theodorou.
        p.   cm.—(Remarkable world)
    Includes bibliographical references (p.   –)and index.
    Summary: Describes the characteristics of different
kinds of dinosaurs explaining their habits and
environment and what may have caused their extinction.
    ISBN 1-56847-415-6 (alk. paper)
    1. Dinosaurs—Juvenile literature. [1. Dinosaurs.]
I. Title. II. Series.
QE862.D5T4735   1996
567.9'1—dc20   95-40607

Printed in Italy

Picture acknowledgments
American Museum of Natural History 25b; Ann Ronan/Image
Select 34r, 35b, 37r; BFI Stills, Posters and Designs 18; Brigham
Young University 10; Natural History Museum, London *front
cover (right)*/John Sibbick, *front cover (left)*, *front cover
(bottom)*, 1/John Sibbick, 4, 5r/John Sibbick, 6-7/John Sibbick,
8l/John Sibbick, 9t, 11t/John Sibbick, 11b, 12-13, 13t, 14t/John
Sibbick, 14b, 15/John Sibbick, 16t, 17/John Sibbick, 19 all, 20
both, 21/John Sibbick, 22 both/John Sibbick, 23, 24/Orbis, 25l,
26 both, 27/John Sibbick, 28/John Sibbick, 29 both/John Sibbick,
30t, 31 both, 32b, 32-33/John Sibbick, 33b, 34b, 35t, 36/John
Sibbick, , 37t, 38, 39t, 40 both, 41/John Sibbick, 45/John Sibbick;
Zefa 6/Colin Maher, 42, 43t/R Cassell, 44. The artwork is by
Peter Bull 7b, 43b; and Tony Townsend 5t, 8r, 9b, 16b, 24b,
30b, 39b.

CONTENTS

Day of the Dinosaur

WHAT would it have been like to live when dinosaurs ruled the earth? Nothing can really show you. You have to use your imagination.

Imagine feeling the ground shake under your feet as a herd of 10,000 *Triceratops* stampedes toward you. Imagine the sound of a 5-ton duck-billed dinosaur calling to its mate with its long, trombonelike head crest. Imagine the sight and smell of a herd of 40-ton *Brachiosaurus* in a conifer forest, pine needles showering down from their munching mouths 50 feet above you.

Right The changing shape of *Iguanodon*. When Victorian scientists first found remains of *Iguanodon*, they rebuilt it as a lumbering monster with a spike on its nose. Modern scientists placed the bony spike correctly on the thumb, but still gave *Iguanodon* an awkward, plodding body. Only very recently has it been seen as a much faster, more active creature.

Left *Tyrannosaurus* is the mightiest example of the dinosaur success story. No modern animal would be a match for this huge predator, which was armed with up to 60 daggerlike teeth as long as six inches.

Dinosaurs lived millions of years ago, long before humans existed. The first scientists who studied the fossil bones of dinosaurs thought dinosaurs must have been giant, cold-blooded reptiles. They saw them as slow-moving, stupid mistakes of nature that died out to make room for the superior mammals. Recent discoveries have shattered this view.

We now know that dinosaurs were a great success. Unlike sluggish modern reptiles, some stood firmly on strong legs that helped them run quickly and supported their huge bodies. Some were small and weighed only a few pounds, while others were as large as whales.

Many of the dinosaurs, like *Ornithomimus* shown here, were fast-moving animals with fairly large brains.

Dinosaur names

The names of dinosaurs and other prehistoric creatures can be hard to say. Here is a pronunciation guide:

Allosaurus *Al-oh-sore-us*
Ankylosaurus *An-kee-low-sore-us*
Apatosaurus *Ah-pat-oh-sore-us*
Archaeopteryx *Ark-ee-opt-er-icks*
Baryonyx *Bar-ee-on-icks*
Brachiosaurus *Brack-ee-oh-sore-us*
Coelophysis *Seel-oh-fie-sis*
Coelurus *Seel-ure-us*
Compsognathus *Komp-sog-nay-thus*
Deinocheirus *Dine-oh-kire-us*
Deinonychus *Dine-oh-nie-kus*
Dimorphodon *Die-more-foe-don*
Diplodocus *Dip-low-dok-us*
Euoplocephalus *You-op-low-keff-ah-lus*
Ichthyosaurus *Ick-thee-oh-sore-us*
Iguanodon *Ig-waa-noh-don*
Kronosaurus *Kron-oh-sore-us*
Lambeosaurus *Lam-bee-oh-sore-us*
Maiasaura *My-ah-sore-ah*
Mamenchisaurus *Mah-men-kee-sore-us*

Ornithomimus *Or-ni-tho-mime-us*
Orodromeus *Ore-oh-drom-ee-us*
Oviraptor *Oh-vee-rap-tor*
Pachycephalosaurus *Pack-ee-seff-ah-low-sore-us*
Panoplosaurus *Pan-oh-ploh-sore-us*
Parasaurolophus *Par-ah-sore-oh-low-fus*
Psittacosaurus *Sit-ack-oh-sore-us*
Pteranodon *Teh-rah-noh-don*
Pterodactylus *Teh-roh-dack-tie-lus*
Pterodaustro *Teh-roh-dow-stroh*
Quetzalcoatlus *Kwet-zal-co-art-lus*
Rhamphorhynchus *Ram-foe-rink-us*
Seismosaurus *Size-moh-sore-us*
Shonisaurus *Shon-ee-sore-us*
Stegoceras *Steg-oh-sair-ass*
Stegosaurus *Steg-oh-sore-us*
Tenontosaurus *Ten-on-toe-sore-us*
Therizinosaurus *Theh-ree-zin-oh-sore-us*
Triceratops *Try-sair-ah-tops*
Tyrannosaurus *Tie-ran-oh-saur-us*
Ultrasaurus *Ul-trah-sore-us*
Utahraptor *You-tah-rap-tor*
Velociraptor *Vel-oss-ee-rap-tor*

Many dinosaurs were probably warm-blooded, fast, and agile. Some were small-brained, but others may have been fairly intelligent. Some lived in family groups, took care of their young, and could communicate by calling to one another or by display. Many may have been brightly colored like modern reptiles or birds.

Dinosaurs ruled the earth for millions of years. They covered every part of the planet, nesting in colonies, living in vast herds, and eating huge quantities of plants—or each other, while their reptile cousins filled the skies and seas.

While the dinosaurs lived and flourished, no mammal bigger than a cat walked the earth. These furry, warm-blooded mammals were our ancestors. Unable to compete with the dinosaurs, they hid in holes and burrows, only coming out at night to feed. They had to wait in the shadows until disaster struck down the mighty dinosaurs.

A dinosaur's footprint fossilized in sandstone. Fossils help scientists figure out what dinosaurs looked like and how they moved.

What is a fossil?

A fossil is the remains of an animal or plant. Dead animals were usually eaten by other animals or decayed in time, leaving no remains. But sometimes a dead animal got buried under sediments—sand, mud, or ash. Although most of the body rotted away, the hard parts, such as bones and teeth, sometimes remained. Over time, they became petrified, or turned to stone, by minerals dissolved in water that seeped in through the surrounding rocks and sediments.

Fossils take millions of years to form and are very rare. We find fossils of plants and animals—and even of footprints. Some fossil leaves show the teeth marks where a dinosaur took a bite.

Rebuilding dinosaurs

Fossil bones are usually found scattered in pieces. Scientists have to rebuild the skeleton. It is like doing a jigsaw puzzle with most of the pieces missing. Once the skeleton has been rebuilt, scientists figure out where muscles were attached to the bones. Finally they can build a model of the whole dinosaur. You have probably seen hundreds of models and drawings of dinosaurs, but the truth is that no one knows exactly what they looked like. Only a tiny amount of dinosaur skin has ever been found, and we still have no idea what color dinosaurs were.

The dinosaur world

The Earth the dinosaurs ruled was much warmer and wetter than it is today. Even the winters were warm. Lush tropical forests stretched for thousands of miles. Ferns and horsetails covered the ground, while above them tall conifers and cycads swayed in the humid breeze. Huge insects buzzed through the air, and the lakes and rivers teemed with frogs and turtles. With a warm climate and a plentiful supply of food, dinosaurs spread from pole to pole. Humans have existed for less than four million years, but for 160 million years dinosaurs were the rulers of the earth.

Allosaurus, a two-ton meat-eater, lived in North America, Africa, Asia, and Australia. It is shown here trying to catch an *Archaeopteryx*, a bird that may have developed from dinosaurs.

Dinosaurs covered the globe. This map shows where their fossils have been found.

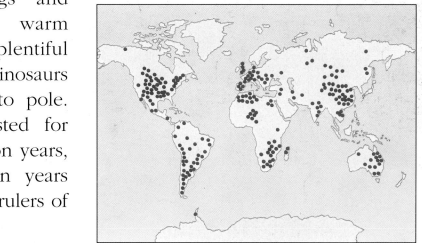

THE BIGGEST DINOSAUR

As well as a long neck, *Brachiosaurus* had high shoulders, which helped it reach twice as high as a modern giraffe.

DINOSAURS came in an amazing variety of sizes. Some, like *Compsognathus*, were only as big as chickens. The biggest of all were the long-necked sauropods. These herbivores were the largest animals that have ever walked the earth. The sauropods had neck ligaments like thick steel cables, but their heads were amazingly small and light. The neck could raise the head like a crane to feed on plentiful palm and conifer trees at heights that no other herbivore, or plant-eater, could reach. Like walking food factories, they ate from dawn until dusk and could strip whole forests bare.

Some sauropods were long and slender. *Diplodocus* was 90 feet long and weighed five times as much as an elephant, but its head was no bigger than a horse's.

Some scientists believe that *Diplodocus* could rear up on its hind legs to raise its head even higher into the trees. Its tiny, peg-like teeth were blunt and probably used to pull leaves off, not to slice them.

Compsognathus (left) was one of the smallest dinosaurs. It was about 30 inches long—most of that neck and tail—and probably weighed less than a big rooster. *Ornitholestes* (center) was about six feet long. Its name means "bird robber," and it probably ate small, fast birds.

This *Diplodocus* skull shows its slender, pine-plucking teeth.

Other sauropods were real heavyweights. The massive *Apatosaurus* (which was previously known as *Brontosaurus*) was not as long as *Diplodocus*, but it was three times heavier, weighing as much as 35 tons. With its thicker, spoon-shaped teeth it could tackle the coarsest leaves and twigs.

Even these giants were dwarfed by mighty *Brachiosaurus*. This huge animal was up to 75 feet from nose to tail and as tall as a five-story building. An adult human would not even have been able to reach up to its knee.

Brachiosaurus's front legs were longer than its back legs, so it looked like a giant giraffe. This huge, 50-ton dinosaur might have lived to a great age—possibly more than 120 years old.

Brachiosaurus had nostrils on the top of its head, which may have helped it to keep its body cool. The large holes at the top of its skull look very similar to the holes on elephant skulls where the trunk fits. Some scientists have suggested that *Brachiosaurus* may have had a trunk, but no fossil evidence has been found to support this.

Below *Diplodocus* (left) was about 90 feet from nose to tail. *Apatosaurus* (center) was 20 feet shorter but, at about 30 tons, was three times as heavy as *Diplodocus*. Both of these giants—and their 50-ton relative *Brachiosaurus*—would have dwarfed humans. However, the dinosaurs died out more than 60 million years before the first humanlike animals evolved.

Super-sauropods

For years, scientists thought that Brachiosaurus *was the largest dinosaur, but in the 1970s a paleontologist named Jim Jensen proved them wrong. In 1972, searching for fossils in Western Colorado, he discovered a few bones from an even bigger brachiosaur-like dinosaur, which he nicknamed* Supersaurus. *Seven years later Jensen found bones from another huge dinosaur,* Ultrasaurus. *This incredibly large sauropod may have weighed as much as 150 tons. In 1984 yet another super-sauropod was found, this time in New Mexico.* Seismosaurus, *or "Earthshaker," may have been a giant relative of* Diplodocus. *Scientists think it may have measured 157 feet, making it the longest animal of all time.*

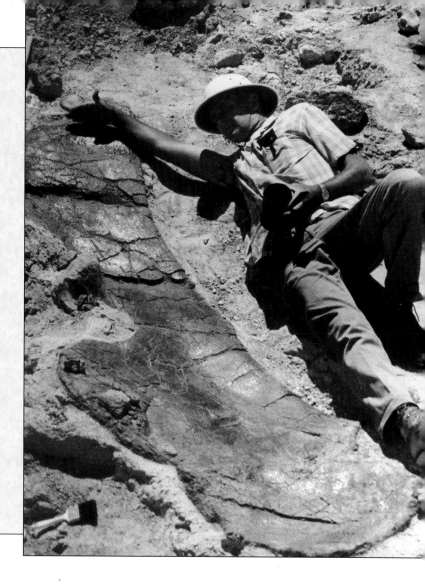

Above Fossil-hunter Jim Jensen lies next to the massive shoulder bone of *Supersaurus*.

Race for the treetops

Why did these "long necks" grow so big? The answer is simple—they were hungry! Competition for food was fierce in Jurassic times, between 208 and 145 million years ago. Medium-sized dinosaurs, like the stegosaurs, could crop ferns and horsetails or rear up on two legs to feed from low-growing branches. Above them was the most plentiful food supply of all: huge conifer trees, bristling with needles and cones. All this energy-giving food remained untouched until the development of the sauropods.

Right This picture shows, from left to right, *Ultrasaurus*, *Brachiosaurus*, and *Supersaurus*. These giants made the ground shake as they walked.

The long, graceful necks of these creatures stretched three times higher than the neck of a giraffe. There was great competition for food among the sauropods. The longer the neck, the more leaves could be reached. As a result, sauropods grew bigger and bigger, with huge stomachs to digest the unending supply of food.

The great neck of China

Mamenchisaurus, *a dinosaur that lived in what is now China, had the longest neck of any animal that has ever lived. Unlike other sauropods,* Mamenchisaurus's *neck was stiff.* Mamenchisaurus *may have stood on its back legs to feed, using its neck like a telegraph pole to raise its head high into the treetops.*

Mamenchisaurus is the largest dinosaur to have been discovered in China. Scientists still do not know why its neck was so long and straight.

THE MOST DANGEROUS DINOSAUR

TYRANNOSAURUS REX was the largest hunter ever to walk the earth. It had forward-facing eyes to spot its prey; long, powerful legs to chase it; and a huge, expandable mouth to swallow another creature in one gulp.

King of killers

What kind of dinosaur was *Tyrannosaurus*? Scientists cannot agree. Some think that it looked far more fearsome than it really was.

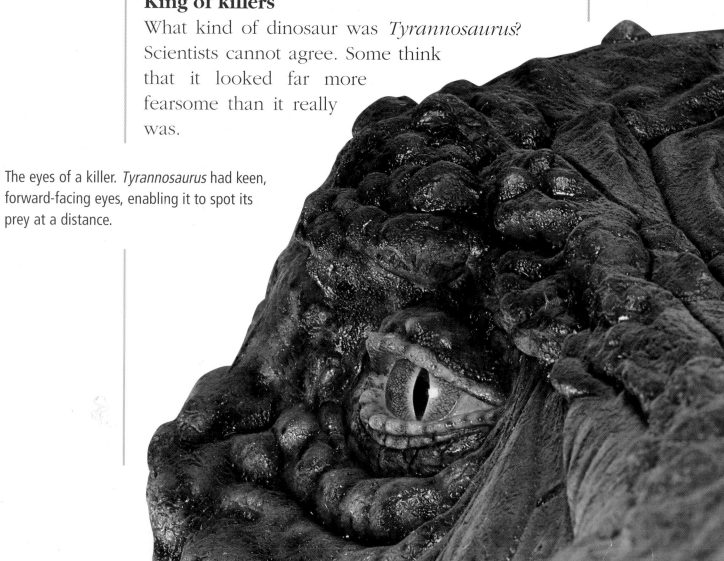

The eyes of a killer. *Tyrannosaurus* had keen, forward-facing eyes, enabling it to spot its prey at a distance.

It was about 18 feet tall and weighed 10 tons. Some scientists believe that *Tyrannosaurus* was too heavy to run or hunt. They think it waddled along like a giant duck, sniffing the air for the smell of a dead dinosaur. It would then feed off the carcass, scaring off the smaller hunters who had made the kill.

However, recent evidence shows that *Tyrannosaurus* was probably more than just a waddling scavenger. It had the long leg bones, strong knee joints, and massive thigh muscles of a fast runner, such as an ostrich. Its eyes were designed like those of an eagle, and it had a large brain.

Tyrannosaurus's jaw had flexible hinges that let it take huge bites out of its prey.

Three of the largest meat-eating dinosaurs—*Tyrannosaurus* (left), *Albertosaurus* (center), and *Daspletosaurus* (right). All three were probably fearsome hunters, but they may also have been scavengers.

Its S-shaped neck was incredibly muscular and its skull was far more solidly built than those of other meat-eaters. All this suggests a fast-running, intelligent hunter, able to sprint after its prey. Its mouth could have delivered a fearsome bite, while its strong skull was able to withstand high-speed clashes with its prey.

How did this super-predator hunt? We can tell from the footprints of other meat-eaters. Fossil dinosaur tracks are quite common. Footprints of plant-eaters are usually found in large groups, but those of the big meat-eaters are nearly always found alone.

Tyrannosaurus would have had to be fast on its feet to dodge the lethal horns of *Triceratops*.

Tyrannosaurus probably hunted alone, rather than in packs. A lone hunter has to be immensely strong. Tyrannosaurus probably followed the huge grazing herds of duckbills and horned dinosaurs, just as modern lions follow zebra or wildebeest. It would pick off the weaker members of a herd—the young, old, and sick.

Earlier meat-eaters such as Allosaurus had large arms with claws. Why did Tyrannosaurus, the biggest of all the meat-eaters, have such tiny, two-clawed arms? Despite its huge size, Tyrannosaurus had to face the biggest, most powerful herbivores of all time. Dinosaurs such as Triceratops or Ankylosaurus had horns and spikes that could fatally injure a predator. To fight such animals, Tyrannosaurus had to be fast and agile enough to run and dodge quickly and then to counterattack with its powerful, crushing bites.

The huge carnivore Allosaurus could have brought down a young Diplodocus. It probably attacked with its fearsome mouth and large, clawed arms.

Big arms would only have slowed *Tyrannosaurus* down and could have gotten injured in a fight. *Tyrannosaurus* was the ultimate in predator design: It sacrificed its arms to develop a fast, powerful bite.

Small but very deadly, *Deinonychus* had grasping hands and vicious kicking claws.

Predator packs

Tyrannosaurus rex may have been the biggest of the meat-eaters, but it was not the most ferocious. There was a dinosaur that was faster than a horse, agile as a cat, had excellent eyesight, and was armed with deadly teeth and claws. Imagine being hunted by a pack of these animals—fast, intelligent, and hungry!

Deinonychus was about ten feet long and could rip its prey to pieces in seconds. On its second toe was a large, curved claw. This was drawn back off the ground when the animal was walking or running, so that it would never get blunt.

First toe

Second toe

"Terrible claw"

Fourth toe

Third toe

The name *Deinonychus* means "terrible claw." The second toe on each of the back feet had a long claw that could be flicked forward to penetrate deep into the flesh of its prey.

16

When attacking a victim, *Deinonychus* could flick the claw forward in an arc and use it as a slashing, tearing weapon.

The discovery of *Deinonychus* proved to scientists that not all dinosaurs were slow, stupid creatures. *Deinonychus* was a superbly designed animal, in many ways superior to modern mammals. It also had an unusually large brain. Such an intelligent dinosaur may have lived in packs, following herds of plant-eaters for prey.

Deinonychus did not need to chase its prey for hours to wear it down, as wolves do. This predator had fast, ostrich-like legs that allowed it to run as fast as a cheetah.

Cheetahs, however, have small teeth and claws and can attack only medium-sized prey.

By hunting in packs, *Deinonychus* was able to attack much larger herbivores, such as this *Tenontosaurus*.

Deinonychus was equipped to kill plant-eaters many times its size. As well as switchblade claws, it had long, strong arms with huge, clawed hands. Its tail was strengthened with bony rods so that it stood out straight and acted like a tightrope-walker's pole. It helped *Deinonychus* keep its balance as it leaped from foot to foot, slashing out at its victim to inflict terrible, bleeding wounds.

A scene from
Jurassic Park

The super-raptor

When planning his dinosaur movie *Jurassic Park*, director Steven Spielberg wanted to cast a sickle-clawed raptor dinosaur as the main villain. He wanted a creature that was larger than any known raptor, so he invented a new "super-raptor" for the film. It was based on an enlarged version of *Deinonychus* and was called, somewhat confusingly, a *Velociraptor*.

New discoveries of large meat-eaters are extremely rare. Yet in a bizarre coincidence, just a few months after the film was made, scientists digging for fossils in Utah found a sickle-shaped claw bigger than anything known before. It belonged to a dinosaur, which was named *Utahraptor*. It was about 20 feet long—twice the size of *Deinonychus*. The scientists had discovered the very dinosaur the filmmakers had invented!

This model was based on the fossilized *Baryonyx* that was found in England in 1983. It shows how scientists think the dinosaur may have looked just after its death.

Claws

When William Walker cracked open a rock in a claypit in Surrey, England, in 1983, he did not realize that he had made one of the most exciting fossil finds of that decade. He was holding pieces of the claw bone of a totally unknown dinosaur.

Baryonyx walkeri was clearly a large, meat-eating dinosaur with a mouth full of sharp teeth. But it had a strangely narrow snout with weak jaws that were more similar to those of a crocodile than of a tyrannosaur. It also had powerful arms and two huge claws shaped more like hooks than blades. The dinosaur puzzled scientists. It was too big and heavy to cut and slash like a raptor, yet its jaws were too weak to bite like a tyrannosaur.

One vital clue helped scientists to find the solution. Inside *Baryonyx*'s rib cage were the remains of its final meal: fish scales.

Baryonyx (bottom left) had jaws very similar to those of a modern crocodile (below). It may have been a fish-eating predator.

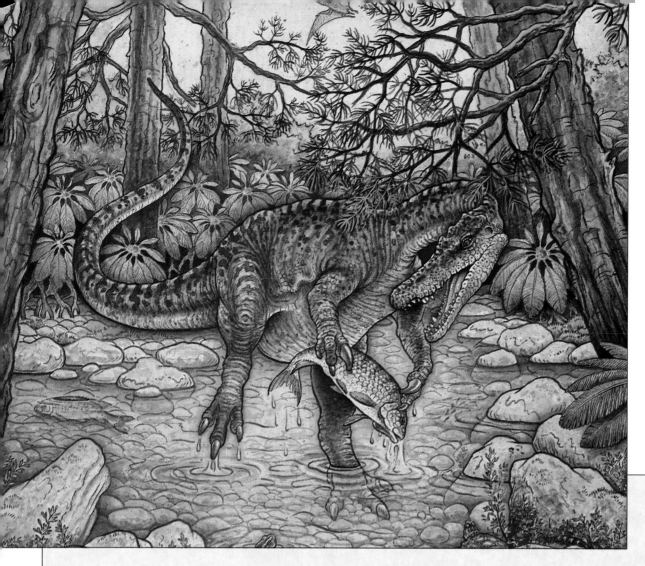

It is not known if *Baryonyx*'s claws were on its hands or its feet. It may have used them as hooks to catch fish in rivers or swamps.

Baryonyx's lucky escape

In January 1983 a bulldozer was digging up clay to make into bricks in a pit in Surrey, England. It exposed the fossil bones of a 120-million-year-old dinosaur. An amateur fossil hunter, William Walker, spotted pieces of the fossil bones and took them home. Once he had stuck them together, he realized he was holding a huge claw—without its tip. He returned to the claypit, but could not remember where he had found the bones. Incredibly he managed to find the exact spot again and recovered the rest of the claw. His son-in-law took the claw to London's Natural History Museum. The scientists there had never seen anything like it. An expedition was sent to the claypit and the complete dinosaur was dug out. They decided to name the dinosaur after Walker—after all, if it hadn't been for him, Baryonyx walkeri would have been made into bricks!

William Walker holding the enormous killing claw of the dinosaur that was named after him

The mysterious giant

Tyrannosaurus might have been the biggest meat-eater ever to have lived, but there is one other mysterious creature of a similar size.

In the late 1920s, in the deserts of Mongolia, scientists discovered the remains of a huge dinosaur. Only its arms were found, but these are more than seven feet long with three huge, curved claws. They called the creature *Deinocheirus,* which means "terrible hand," and imagined it to be a predator that even *Tyrannosaurus* would have feared.

Although huge, *Deinocheirus*'s arms were also very slender, similar to the forearms of dinosaurs called ornithomimosaurs. These are ostrich-like dinosaurs with toothless beaks. They fed on buds, leaves, and possibly smaller dinosaurs and lizards. *Deinocheirus* may have been a giant, plant-eating ornithomimosaur. However, its clawed talons are slightly different than those of most ornithomimosaurs. They seem more suited to ripping flesh than plucking buds. Perhaps *Deinocheirus* was an ostrich-like dinosaur that increased its meat-eating habits and became a terrifying predator.

Struthiomimus was a typical ostrich-like dinosaur. Perhaps the mysterious giant *Deinocheirus* was an enormous relative.

21

HOW PLANT-EATERS DEFENDED THEMSELVES

As predators grew bigger and more fearsome, herbivores had to fight back. Over millions of years, some species of herbivores developed protective armor and defensive spikes and clubs on their bodies. Signs of the battles fought between these armed giants can be found in the scars, teeth marks, and break lines on fossil bones.

Nodosaurs like *Polacanthus* (front), *Hylaeosaurus* (left), and *Nodosaurus* (right) were all protected with bony-plated armor.

Armored vegetarians

The most fearsome plant-eaters of all time must have been the horned dinosaurs. The biggest of them all was *Triceratops*. It weighed more than an African bull elephant and could run faster than a rhinoceros.

The most dangerously armed herbivore of all time. This baby *Triceratops* was very well protected by its fearsome parent.

These ten-ton monsters roamed the world in great herds, like wildebeest across the plains of Africa.

Many *Triceratops* fossils have been found, so we know they were very successful animals. It isn't difficult to see why. With fast, strong legs, powerful neck muscles, and the heaviest skull of any land animal, these dinosaurs were built to charge. Their horns grew up to 40 inches long and pointed straight ahead, just above their eyes. Like jousting knights on horseback, they could charge headfirst at the soft belly of a tyrannosaur.

Triceratops relied on its fearsome horns to tackle predators. Other plant-eaters developed full body armor as a defense. The nodosaurs were covered in solid, bony panels. Predators would have broken their teeth on this thick armor plating. Only the bellies of the nodosaurs were unprotected.

Dinosaur development

It's thought that the horned dinosaurs developed from small, agile, two-legged "parrot" dinosaurs. The parrot dinosaurs had strong jaw muscles to help them chew tough plants. The jaw muscles were anchored to a thick ridge of bone at the back of the skull. In time, this may have grown into a crest, which males would use for display. Their bodies also became more massive, to support bigger and bigger stomachs. After millions of years these small, timid parrot dinosaurs had developed into huge, horned beasts that could fend off any predator on earth.

The ancestors of *Triceratops* probably looked like the parrot dinosaur *Psittacosaurus* (left) and the piglike *Protoceratops*.

23

With their short legs and wide, squat bodies, nodosaurs were built like massive Sumo wrestlers. It would have been difficult for a predator to knock down a 4.5-ton nodosaur. To add to these defenses, nodosaurs like *Panoplosaurus* had huge, sharp spikes on each shoulder. It could shoulder-charge an attacker, slicing at the predator's legs with its shoulder-spikes.

The ankylosaurs were also heavily armored, but they had an even more deadly surprise weapon. At the end of an ankylosaur's tail was a huge, two-headed club made of bone. Massive muscles ran up the tail to help an ankylosaur swing this war club with enormous power. An attacking tyrannosaur would have had to move with great agility to avoid the bone-cracking club swings or the jagged spikes along the ankylosaur's body.

There was plenty of meat on the large, squat body of *Ankylosaurus*, but any hungry *Tyrannosaurus* risked a bone-shattering blow from its clubbed tail.

The skeleton of the ankylosaur *Euoplocephalus*. It was well protected, with a heavily armored head, strongly built legs, and a large tail club. *Euoplocephalus* measured about 20 feet from nose to tail.

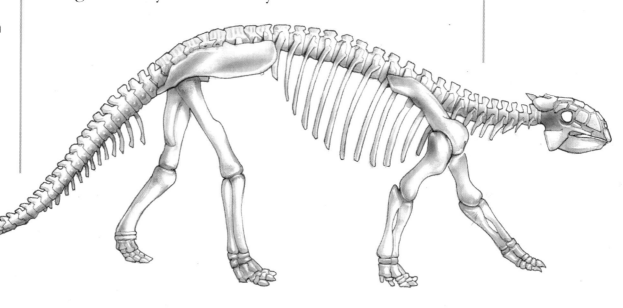

Although the ankylosaur's war club was a fearsome weapon, the most destructive tail of all time belonged to *Stegosaurus.* Although it was probably a timid plant-eater, if attacked *Stegosaurus* could wield a muscular tail that ended with spikes covered in sharp horn. These spikes grew up to three feet long and could inflict terrible injuries. With its huge back legs and much shorter front legs, *Stegosaurus* was built to spin around in quick turns, protecting its tiny head with its thrashing killer tail.

Unarmed dinosaurs

How did the gentle sauropods defend themselves from predators as big as elephants? One answer must be their sheer size. A huge, charging *Brachiosaurus* could have crushed any big meat-eater under its feet. Some scientists also believe that sauropods like *Apatosaurus* had very powerful jaws. An adult could possibly have delivered a crushing bite to an unwary predator.

More slender sauropods, such as *Diplodocus,* had very weak jaws, but they may have had a surprise for an attacker in their tails.

An *Allosaurus* prepares to attack an *Apatosaurus.* This drawing is based on fossil footprints found at Glen Rose, Texas.

Fossil footprints found at Glen Rose. The large *Apatosaurus* tracks can be seen next to those of a three-toed predator.

25

The last yard or so of *Diplodocus*'s massive, muscular tail was made of long, bony rods. Some scientists believe that *Diplodocus* could have lashed at attackers with its whip-tipped tail and knocked them to the ground.

Prehistoric battering rams

Dome-headed dinosaurs, from left to right, *Stegoceras*, *Pachycephalosaurus*, and *Homalocephale*.

Dome-headed dinosaurs, such as *Stegoceras* and *Pachycephalosaurus*, had no body armor or horns, but they did have extraordinary skulls, which could have been up to ten inches thick on the top. These may have developed in ramming contests between males, but they may also have been used for defense. When the dinosaurs charged, their domed heads probably acted like a massive boxing glove, cracking the ribs of a predator.

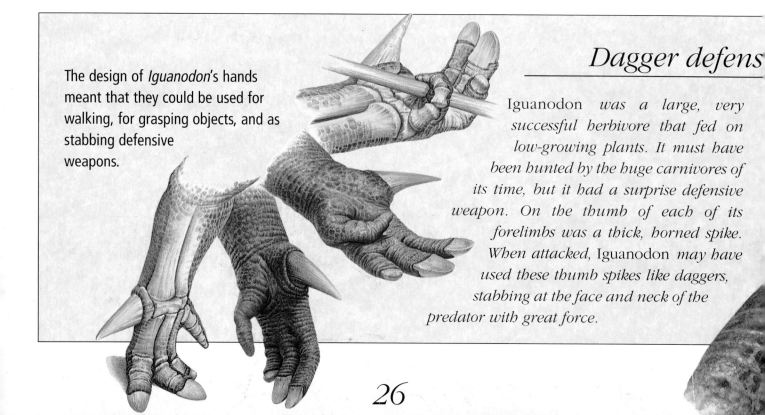

The design of *Iguanodon*'s hands meant that they could be used for walking, for grasping objects, and as stabbing defensive weapons.

Dagger defens

Iguanodon was a large, very successful herbivore that fed on low-growing plants. It must have been hunted by the huge carnivores of its time, but it had a surprise defensive weapon. On the thumb of each of its forelimbs was a thick, horned spike. When attacked, Iguanodon *may have used these thumb spikes like daggers, stabbing at the face and neck of the predator with great force.*

Iguanodon's thumb spikes, together with its very strong arms, could have pierced the skin of the toughest attacker.

DINOSAUR HERDS

SCIENTISTS used to think that dinosaurs were too stupid to live in family groups. But in 1989, millions of fossil dinosaur tracks were uncovered in the Rocky Mountains. The tracks showed that huge numbers of one species of dinosaurs had walked together in the same direction on a prehistoric "highway" along what was the shoreline of an ancient sea. This was clear proof that some dinosaurs did live together in huge herds, and that they may have migrated to warmer lands to find food.

Many other trackways have also been found. One set of sauropod tracks seems to show that the big adults walked on the outside of the herd to protect the younger ones in the middle.

These three groups of hadrosaurs—*Parasaurolophus* (left), *Corythosaurus* (center foreground), and *Lambeosaurus* (right)—can sense the approach of a predator.

Other fossil evidence supports the idea of dinosaur herds. Mass fossil graves have been found, where an entire herd was overcome by a dust storm or flash flood. One mass grave in Montana contains over 10,000 *Maiasaura* that were buried in ash during a volcanic eruption.

If many dinosaurs did live in herds, they must have been able to communicate, to recognize members of their family or group, and to compete for mates. How did they do this?

Colorful dinosaurs

One way to communicate is by color. Most animals use color to recognize members of their own species, so it is likely that dinosaurs did the same. Another important reason for skin color is camouflage. Perhaps herbivores were patterned to blend into the forests where they fed. Hunters may also have been camouflaged. Perhaps *Brachiosaurus* was spotted like a giraffe and *Tyrannosaurus* was striped like a tiger!

Dinosaurs may also have used color at mating time. Some scientists believe that male *Triceratops* had bright colors on their frills, which they used for display like peacocks do.

It is not know if dinosaurs were brightly colored or dull. The artist who painted these pictures has given *Lambeosaurus* (top left) and *Parasaurolophus* (left) very distinctive skin markings. *Parasaurolophus* also has a flap of skin attached to its huge crest.

With their heads down, they could have frightened off rival males and attracted females.

The head crest of *Parasaurolophus* was a yard long. Inside was a complicated arrangement of hollow tubes and chambers. Air from the lungs could be blown out through the tubes to produce a low note.

Tsintaosaurus (left rear), *Saurolophus* (in the pool), *Corythosaurus* (right rear), and *Parasaurolophus* (right). Each species of hadrosaur had its own special head crest.

Honking hadrosaurs

Duckbilled dinosaurs, or hadrosaurs, had musical heads! Their head crests were hollow, like musical instruments. At first it was thought that the duckbills used them as snorkels to breathe air while they swam in lakes, but this idea was proved to be wrong when no hole was found at the end of the crests. Most scientists now believe that when the duckbills blew through their noses, their amazing head crests made a loud, low, hooting noise, like a trombone. They may have hooted at each other to choose mates or as a danger signal.

Nests and eggs

Dinosaurs laid eggs, just as crocodiles and turtles do.

Some eggs were round; others were elliptical, with one end narrower than the other. They were laid in nests dug in earth or sand. Hundreds of fossil nests have been found together, proving that herds of dinosaurs nested in huge colonies. They probably returned to the same site every year to nest.

Freshly hatched *Maiasaura* would have been too weak to leave the nest. They would have been easy prey for predators.

Two dome-headed dinosaurs in battle

Dinosaur head-bangers

Dome-headed dinosaurs, such as Pachycephalosaurus, *probably used their super-thick skulls in butting contests to choose a mate. Like massive rams, the males must have stood face to face pawing the ground and snorting. Then they sprinted toward each other and crashed heads with a bone-crunching thud.*

Nests of the large duckbill *Maiasaura* contain tiny pieces of eggshell. This shows that *Maiasaura* babies probably stayed in the nest for some weeks, crushing the empty eggshells underfoot. Their parents must have protected them and brought them food.

A *Maiasaura* nesting colony must have been an incredible sight. Huge adults would rest by each nest, perhaps pecking at other adults that came too near. Others would come and go with mouthfuls of leaves and berries for their young. Small, scavenging lizards would be hiding in the shadows, waiting for a chance to snatch tiny baby *Maiasaura* from an unguarded nest. The *Maiasaura* may have made loud cries of alarm when the colony was discovered by a predator. But no one knows how these dinosaurs defended their nests from attack.

A *Maiasaura* nesting colony. Adults are thought to have piled plants on top of the nests to keep the eggs warm until they hatched.

Egg-stealer or seed-cracker?

One predator that may have stalked the nesting colonies was Oviraptor. *This small, fast dinosaur may have been adapted for egg-stealing. Its large, long-fingered hands would have been perfect for snatching and holding an egg. Instead of teeth it had two sharp spikes in the roof of its mouth.* Oviraptor *could have clamped its beak around an egg and the spikes would neatly crack the shell, allowing it to lap up the yolk. However, some scientists believe that* Oviraptor*'s mouth might instead have been used to crack open hard fruits and seeds or shellfish.*

Not all dinosaurs were such good parents. Nests of the dinosaur *Orodromeus* contain eggs that were almost intact, except where the baby dinosaur had hatched from the top. This shows that as soon as the babies hatched, they left the nest to find food on their own.

Fossil remains of the dinosaur *Coelophysis* have been found with tiny *Coelophysis* skeletons inside them. It seems that this dinosaur may have eaten its own young.

A *Coelophysis* skeleton with the bones of young *Coelophysis* inside.

REPTILES IN THE OCEANS

DINOSAURS were rulers of the prehistoric land, but other swimming reptiles dominated the seas. These reptiles had once lived on land, but returned to the sea and developed fins and paddles. They had to come to the surface to breathe air, like whales. Some of these marine reptiles were the largest and most fearsome predators ever to have swum the oceans.

Dolphins of the prehistoric seas

Ichthyosaurs were the rulers of the open seas. Skimming beneath the water's surface, leaping and diving between the waves, they could easily have been mistaken for dolphins. These sleek, torpedo-shaped reptiles used their excellent eyesight and great speed to catch fish and squid. They had fishlike tails that moved from side to side, pushing them through the water at speeds that may have reached 30 mph. All modern reptiles lay eggs, but scientists have found fossil evidence to prove that ichthyosaurs gave birth to live young.

With its sleek body, *Ichthyosaurus* was probably the fastest swimmer of its time. Its snapping jaws would have made it a fierce predator.

This drawing, done over a hundred years ago, shows a *Mosasaurus* fighting a long-necked plesiosaur.

Flying swimmers

Although they were not as fast as the ichthyosaurs, plesiosaurs were agile, skillful swimmers. By moving their flippers up and down they swam through the water the way penguins do. With their long necks they could reach out to catch fish or probe around rocks for hidden prey. Shorter-necked plesiosaurs, called pliosaurs, had huge, fanged mouths to hunt larger prey. Like whales and dolphins, Plesiosaurs did not have fins to breathe underwater, and so had to come to the surface to breathe.

Ocean giants

Most ichthyosaurs were dolphin-sized, but some grew much bigger. *Shonisaurus* grew to a massive 50 feet in length. It had teeth only at the front of its huge beak and probably hunted large squid. Large numbers of fossil *Shonisaurus* have been found in the Sierra Nevadas in California, all lying in the same position. A group may have become trapped on a beach and died together.

Even larger was the terrifying *Kronosaurus,* the biggest swimming reptile of all time. This 55-foot pliosaur may have lived like a killer whale, attacking large prey such as giant squid, huge prehistoric turtles, and other swimming reptiles.

Plesiosaurus was a very agile swimmer, darting after small fish and squid.

This skull of a *Mosasaurus* was found in 1780 near Maastricht, the Netherlands. It caused a sensation at the time because it was one of the first fossil skulls to be identified as a prehistoric animal.

REPTILES IN THE SKY

Swooping across the sky and hopping around the shores, flying reptiles such as *Pterodactylus* and *Rhamphorhynchus* were masters of the prehistoric skies.

OVER 70 million years ago, the sky was filled with some of the most fantastic creatures the world has ever known. Some were as small as sparrows, while others were giants measuring half the length of a jumbo jet's wing. They filled the forests, soared high above the oceans and deserts, nested in vast colonies, and fed on plankton, fish, squid, insects, worms, and even dead dinosaurs. These animals were not dinosaurs but were pterosaurs, distant reptile relatives of the dinosaurs.

Unlike modern scaled reptiles, pterosaurs were covered in soft fur and may even have been brightly colored, like birds.

Pteranodon's head crest was a masterpiece of reptile design. Experiments with models in wind tunnels have shown that the crest acted like a weather vane, keeping *Pteranodon* facing into the wind.

One of the biggest and most spectacular of all the pterosaurs was *Pteranodon*. Its wingspan was wider than the length of a bus, yet its body only weighed as much as a three-year-old child. Hollow, air-filled bones helped *Pteranodon* gain size without putting on weight. When *Pteranodon* spread out its huge wings, even gentle breezes would have lifted this giant high into the sky.

When scientists first examined the fossil remains of pterosaurs, they decided that pterosaurs must have been stupid batlike creatures with weak, primitive wings. New fossil discoveries have changed that view. It is now thought that the pterosaurs were expert fliers, with big brains and specialized feeding methods. The small inset picture shows a *Rhamphorhynchus* tooth.

The Texas giant

Measuring over 40 feet from wingtip to wingtip, *Quetzalcoatlus* was the largest flying creature of all time.

For years, scientists thought that Pteranodon was the biggest flying creature of all time. But in 1975, in Big Bend, Texas, fossil bones of an unknown pterosaur of incredible size were discovered. With a head longer than a person and a wingspan the length of two buses, Quetzalcoatlus *stunned the scientific world. Many scientists simply refused to believe that anything so big could have gotten off the ground. Once again they had underestimated reptile design. Although* Quetzalcoatlus *was bigger than some small aircraft, its body weighed as little as an ultralight plane. It would have glided through the warm Cretaceous skies, riding the thermals and air currents with ease.*

Some scientists have suggested that Quetzalcoatlus *lived like a giant vulture. When it spotted a dead dinosaur from high in the sky, it would spiral down and feed on the carcass, sticking its long, snakelike neck deep into the body to reach the soft inner organs. Others believe it was a fish-eater, like* Pteranodon.

Pteranodon probably spent most of its life on the wing, gliding over the oceans like an albatross, snatching up the occasional slow-moving fish.

Amazing heads, beaks, and bills

Every pterosaur had a head designed for a different way of catching and eating food. Like modern birds, they probably used their beaks and bills in mating displays, so some may have been brightly colored.

Pteranodon had no teeth, but it had a huge bill with a pouch of skin under its lower jaw. It used its bill as a net to scoop up fish and swallow them whole, like a pelican. *Dimorphodon* had a thick, powerful beak that could have crushed squid or shelled ammonites. *Rhamphorhynchus* had sharp, protruding teeth that it used to spike fish as it flew above the surface of the sea.

Not all pterosaurs fed on the wing. *Pterodactylus* was a small pterosaur with a long, flexible neck. With its wings folded up, it may have hopped along mud flats or beaches, probing for worms with its long snout.

Rhamphorhynchus's spiky mouth was ideal for spearing fish as it skimmed over the surface of the sea.

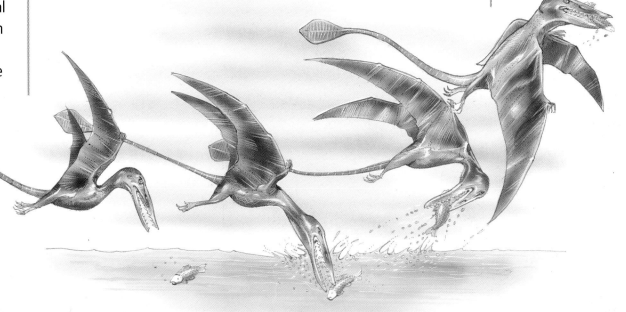

Pink pterosaurs?

One of the most extraordinary beaks ever discovered belongs to Pterodaustro. *Its curved bottom jaw was full of long, thin teeth like bristles. It used this bristle-beak to sieve for tiny shrimps in shallow water like a flamingo. Modern flamingos have white feathers when they are born. They only turn pink because they eat shrimp that contain pink pigment. It is possible that, 200 million years ago, these pterosaurs were also turned pink by their shrimp-rich diet.*

Perhaps *Pterodaustro* was white, like many modern sea birds—or it could have been flamingo pink.

Right A fossil *Archaeopteryx*. It has a reptile-like bony tail and claws on its fingers, as well as the faint impressions made by the feathers on its tail and wings.

Were dinosaurs birds?

In 1861 the fossilized remains of a strange pigeon-sized animal were found. The creature was given the name *Archaeopteryx*. It had a body like a small dinosaur, a head with a beak full of teeth, clawed hands, and a long tail. It was also covered with feathers. Was it a dinosaur or a bird?

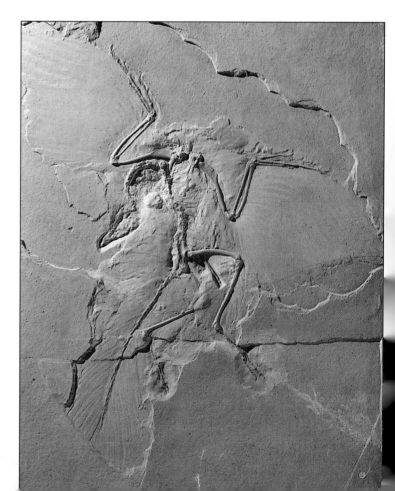

We now know that *Archaeopteryx* was a bird, not a dinosaur, but scientists have different views about how it lived. It did not have the big muscles that birds need to fly. Some scientists think it ran along the ground, using its feathered wings as traps to swat flying insects out of the air.

However, most think it lived in the trees, climbing with its claws and using its wings to glide from branch to branch. Many scientists believe that *Archaeopteryx* is proof that birds developed from small, meat-eating dinosaurs.

Archaeopteryx was probably not a strong flyer, but by gliding among the trees it could have caught slow-moving insects. It may also have been able to run and climb.

THE END OF THE DINOSAURS

DINOSAURS were one of the most successful groups of animals ever to have lived. Yet 64 million years ago a killer struck, wiping them from the face of the earth forever. The great reptiles that ruled the seas and skies were also destroyed. To this day no one has proved the identity of their killer. Scientists have come up with many different theories, but they cannot agree on who is right.

The murderer that struck 64 million years ago did not kill all the life on this planet. It killed the dinosaurs on land, but left the small mammals, lizards, and snakes alive. It killed the flying reptiles—the pterosaurs—but not the birds. It killed the swimming reptiles, such as the plesiosaurs and ichthyosaurs, but not the turtles or the freshwater crocodiles. Many other sea creatures were also wiped out, including the ammonites and huge quantities of tiny plankton. Although many animals died, plants and trees were not badly affected.

The disaster that struck down the dinosaurs also destroyed millions of sea creatures, like these fossilized ammonites.

Death stars?
Two death star theories have been put forward to explain the death of the dinosaurs.

What happened?

Hundreds of reasons have been suggested for the death of the dinosaurs. Here are some very strange theories (which very few scientists still believe):

- *Meat-eating dinosaurs ate all the plant-eaters and then starved to death.*
- *The dinosaurs went blind from cosmic rays and could no longer find their food.*
- *Tiny mammals ate all the dinosaur eggs.*
- *Aliens took the dinosaurs away for food.*
- *The dinosaurs simply lost the will to live and committed suicide.*

One suggests that a distant star exploded, bathing the earth in deadly cosmic rays. But these rays would probably have killed all the birds and mammals as well as the dinosaurs.

The other "Death Star" theory is that our sun has a twin called Nemesis, a dimmer star that orbits the earth once every 26 million years. When it comes close to our solar system, it sends out hundreds of meteorites, comets, and asteroids, which shower down on the earth.

This idea is based on fossil evidence that shows that about every 26 million years many species of animals seem to die out. However, if such a sun existed it would affect the movements of other stars and planets. Astronomers have found no trace of this mystery star.

Does the sun have a mysterious twin? Could this be the path it would take? The Oort Cloud, which is thought to lie beyond the solar system, may be where many comets come from.

Some scientists believe that 64 million years ago, hundreds of volcanoes erupted at once, sending out vast lava flows and poisonous gases that killed the dinosaurs.

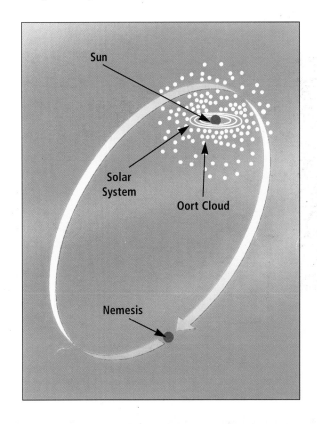

Sun

Solar System

Oort Cloud

Nemesis

This huge crater at Wolf Creek, Australia, was caused by a meteorite hitting the earth.

The world's worst weekend?

When scientists look at rocks that are 64 million years old, they often find a thin layer of red clay. In that clay are traces of a rare metal called iridium, which is often brought to the earth from space in meteorites. Many scientists believe that 64 million years ago a huge meteorite—perhaps six miles across—struck the earth with tremendous force.

The enormous blast would have caused massive tidal waves, violent winds, and earthquakes. The vaporized meteorite would have sent a huge dust cloud into the atmosphere, blotting out the sun for months. Without sunlight, the plants and trees would have shed their leaves and needles, and the plant-eating dinosaurs would have starved to death. Then the meat-eaters would have wasted away. In the sun-starved seas, the plankton would have died. The tiny shrimp and fish that fed on the plankton would have starved, causing the death of the ammonites and the great marine reptiles.

More than one killer?

Perhaps the dinosaurs were killed by more than one event. For about five million years before they died out, the earth's climate was getting cooler. As a result, the dinosaurs could have become weaker and fewer in number. Then massive volcanic activity or a giant meteorite impact may have blotted out the sun. In this long period of darkness, only small animals such as tiny mammals, lizards, and snakes could have survived. The rulers of the earth, the dinosaurs, would have been too big and too hungry to live through the long, dark winter.

If modern birds are the direct descendants of the dinosaurs, then in one sense the great reptiles never did die out.

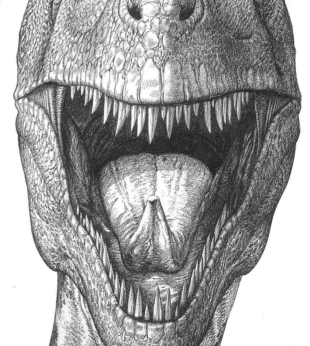

45

Glossary

Ammonites Prehistoric marine creatures with spiral-shaped shells.

Asteroid A lump of rock, between a few inches and a few miles across, that moves around the sun in space.

Camouflaged Patterned or colored in a way that makes something hard to see against its background.

Carcass The dead body of an animal.

Carnivores Animals that eat only meat.

Catastrophe A terrible disaster.

Cold-blooded A cold-blooded animal has to spend as much time as possible in the sun in order to keep warm, because it cannot regulate its own body temperature. Modern reptiles are cold blooded.

Comet A small object, made of ice and dust, that travels around the sun in space.

Conifers Trees with needles and cones, such as pines and firs.

Cretaceous The period in the earth's history between 145 million and 64 million years ago.

Cycad A type of plant that was common at the time of the dinosaurs.

Herbivores Animals that eat only plants.

Jurassic The period in the earth's past from about 208 million to 145 million years ago.

Ligaments The fibers in an animal's body that connect bones and muscles.

Long-necks A nickname for sauropod dinosaurs.

Mammal A warm-blooded animal that produces live young and feeds them on milk from the mother.

Meteorite A rocklike object that falls from space onto the surface of the earth or another planet or a moon.

Orbit The curved path taken by a planet as it moves around the sun or by a moon moving around a planet.

Paleontologist A scientist who studies fossils.

Predator An animal that kills and eats other animals.

Protruding Sticking out.

Scavenger An animal that feeds on the remains of dead animals it finds, rather than on prey it has killed.

Sediment Particles of rock and soil that settle on the bed of a river, lake, or sea. Over millions of years, as sediments build up, those at the bottom can be squeezed together to form rock.

Thermals Currents of warm air that move up through cooler surrounding air.

Ultralight plane A very small aircraft, like a hang glider powered by a gasoline engine.

Vaporize The changing of something into a gas or a sudden disappearance.

FURTHER INFORMATION

BOOKS

Barnes-Svarney, Patricia L. *Fossils: Stories from Stones and Bones*. Earth Processes. Springfield, NJ: Enslow Publishers, 1991.

Benton, Mike. *How Do We Know Dinosaurs Existed?* How Do We Know? Milwaukee: Raintree Steck-Vaughn, 1995.

Cohen, Daniel. *Allosaurus and Other Jurassic Meat-Eaters*. Dinosaurs of North America. Danbury, CT: Childrens Press, 1995.

Dixon, Dougal. *The Search for Dinosaurs*. Digging up the Past. New York: Thomson Learning, 1995.

Farlow, James O. *On the Tracks of Dinosaurs: A Study of Dinosaur Footprints*. Prehistoric Creatures. New York: Franklin Watts, 1991.

Lambert, David and Wright, Rachel. *Dinosaurs*. Craft Topics. New York: Franklin Watts, 1992.

Liptak, Karen. *Dating Dinosaurs and Other Old Things*. Brookfield, CT: Millbrook Press, 1992.

Nardo, Don. *The Extinction of the Dinosaurs*. Exploring the Unknown. San Diego: Lucent Books, 1994.

Parker, Steve. *Dinosaurs and How They Lived*. New York: Dorling Kindersley, 1991.

Pearce, Q.L. *Tyrannosaurus Rex and Other Dinosaur Wonders*. Amazing Science. New York: Julian Messner, 1990.

Stein, Wendy. *Dinosaurs*. Opposing Viewpoints Great Mysteries. San Diego: Greenhaven Press, 1994.

The Visual Dictionary of Dinosaurs. Eyewitness Visual Dictionaries. New York: Dorling Kindersley, 1992.

VIDEOTAPES

Dinosaur! (Televideo) An exciting series of four vidotapes, narrated by Walter Cronkite, that includes animated sequences of robotic model dinosaurs.

Jurassic Park (Columbia Tristar Video) Steven Spielberg's blockbuster about living dinosaurs recreated from fossil remains by modern scientists—with terrifying results.

CD-ROMS

Microsoft Dinosaurs A huge amount of information—more than 1,000 color illustrations and photos, 1,300 articles and 6 animated movies—presented in a highly entertaining way.

Smithsonian Institute's Dinosaur Museum An informative collection of dinosaur facts and figures, including a dictionary, dinosaur myths, plenty of photos, and some games to play.

Grolier Prehistoria An introduction to prehistoric life from its first appearance on earth, with lots of facts, short videos and illustrations of over five hundred creatures.

You may also wish to join the Dinosaur Society, which publishes a monthly newsletter called *DinoTimes*. For more information write to The Dinosaur Society, 200 Carleton Avenue, East Islip, NY 11730.

INDEX